MONET

BY YVON TAILLANDIER

THE UFFICI PRESS - LUGANO

Title page: EDOUARD MANET
Monet's Floating Studio (Detail), 1874
Oil 30" × 40"
Bayerische Staatsgalerie, Munich

Translated from the French by:
A. P. H. HAMILTON

Déjeuner sur ~~~~~~~~~~~~~~~ ~~nic Lunch) (Detail), 1866. Oil 164" × 59" Louvre, Paris

FATHER OF THE IMPRESSIONISTS

There are sounds of waves, of oars in the water and of leaves shimmering.
Rays from the sun strike the jacket of a stroller standing under a row of trees whose low-hung branches hide the river from him and trace patterns of light upon his shoulder.
A bearded man in his thirties, stoutish and small of stature, dressed in a white smock and wearing a bell-shaped hat is at the oars. He is not a fisherman about to cast his line into the stream and he is not an oarsman with a passion for rowing, but an artist who, to use a term of the trade is " on his way out to paint ". He has taken his boat out today and has, in all probability, decided to paint the Seine from a point out in the stream. The stroller on the bank has recognised him at once although few people in 1874 would have known

5

much about this artist in his white smock, a real countryman with a penchant for painting water. Nevertheless, an exhibition of paintings, etchings and statuary at Nadar's photographic studio, 35 Boulevard des Capucines, in Paris contained a canvas of his, hung among those of his artist friends with a similar taste in art. The picture has already attracted the eye of a journalist, a neologist, who was later to make a fortune. It is called " An Impression: Sunrise ". The last word of this title, full of symbolic meaning, meant nothing to the journalist who has already forgotten it. He retained only the word " impression " and later invented the word " impressionist ". But, at this time, the word had an unpleasant ring about it, for those to whom it was applied were usually thought of as mad.

Near Argenteuil, the man out strolling has good reasons for not sharing this opinion; but, at the time, he was unaware of it. He is now engrossed in laying down on the grassy bank, a heavy box and a wooden instrument he was carrying over his shoulder, attached to a strap. Then, standing upright again, he shaded his eyes from the fierce summer sun and looked at the boat.

It is a small boat with a little cabin, deck space and a mast. When, later, the artist spoke of his modest vessel, he described it as a barge. It is true that if vessels which once contained well-known personalities were of a size in proportion to the owner's stature, the quality of his work and his role in history, the boat belonging to Claude Monet, the painter in a white smock, would be classed neither as a skiff, nor a barge, but an ocean liner.

Monet has been called "The Raphael of water" and "the inventor of colour". His name might also be given to the discovery of " the moment in time " because of his great contribution to the pictorial representation of moments and the fleeting aspect of nature. His name might also be associated with the painting of light. He can also be classed as a forerunner, not only of his immediate successors the impressionists and neo-impressionists, but also of fauvists, cubists, abstract painters, the non-figurists, painters of mottled and speckled paintings of simple motifs and calligraphic art. He initiated the taste, now widespread amongst artists, for Far Eastern works of art and other oriental disciplines. Some of the aspects of what might be called the representation of space in modern art is already discernable in some of Monet's works. Certain principles of composition which are nowadays quite common and even the creative technique employed by many contemporary artists, are already in the forefront of his mind. He is almost as worthy as Cézanne of the distinction of being " the father of modern art ", but he is more often accorded the honour of being called " the father of the impressionists ".

He was not the senior among the group of impressionists. He was ten years younger than Pissarro, the eldest of them, born in 1830 in the West Indies. Between 1874 and 1886, the Impressionists held eight exhibitions. Monet did not exhibit at the fifth and sixth and final exhibition. Pissarro exhibited at all eight. Dedicated to his work and absorbed in it, Pissarro wrote – " my life is wholly identified with the history of impressionism ". Monet could not aspire to this claim. His absence from the exhibitions could be attributed to the fact that the group, as a whole, did not follow up its original intentions, with the result

Caricature
(M. Orchard), 1896
Pencil Drawing
12¾" × 9½"
Carter H. Harrison
Collection
The Art Institute
of Chicago

that Monet considered Pissarro's adhesion to the group as a lack of faith and that he, Monet, remained untainted and faithful to the original conceptions, entirely uncompromising. Throughout the greater part of their careers, the impressionists had to contend with extreme difficulties of many kinds. The public was violently hostile and sarcastic. They were poor and lived miserably and suffered in their private lives. Renoir once said to his dealer, Ambroise Vollard – "Without Monet, we would all have given up". Monet went further than the other impressionists in capturing the fleeting moment, creating a degree of wooliness in some of his canvases which have not been interpreted with any certainty. He was indeed an extremist.

Monet survived them all. Of the great impressionists, it was he who lived longest. Berthe Morisot died in 1895, Sisley in 1899 and Pissarro in 1903. Renoir died in 1919. During his life, he remained very close to the ideals of impressionism. Other early impressionists were Cézanne and Degas. With Renoir, they remained dissident and critical of contemporary art. While Renoir and Monet were alive in the 20th century, astonishing aesthetic revolutions occured such as fauvism in 1905, cubism in 1908 and dadaism in 1915. In 1924, when the *Surrealist Manifesto* by André Breton appeared, Renoir had died, but Claude Monet was still alive. He died in 1926.

Was the last great impressionist painter, in fact, the first? Did the impressionist school which came to a close with Monet begin with him? He and others, Renoir and Pissarro in particular, originated the impressionists. The first real impressionist paintings dated back to 1869 and were painted by Pissarro round Pontoise and at La Grenouillère, Bougival, near Ver-

Studies, 1864 Jean-Pierre Hoschedé Collection, Giverny

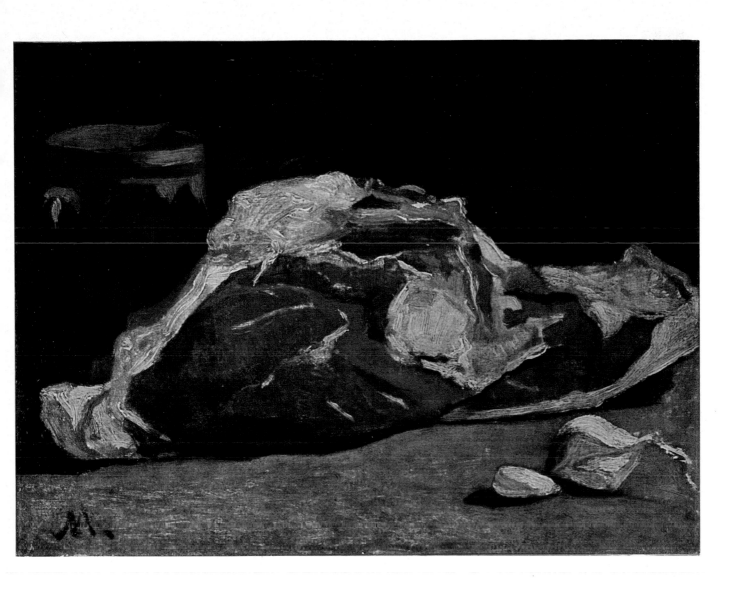

STILL LIFE, The Side of Beef, 1864
Oil 9½″ × 13″. Louvre, Paris

TERRACE AT SAINTE-ADRESSE, 1886
Oil 38½″ × 52″ T. Pitcairn, Bry-Athyn, Pennsylvania

◁

FLOWER GARDEN, 1866
Oil 25½″ × 21″ Louvre, Paris

11

Claude Monet

Portrait of Camille Monet, 1866-67
Drawing. Private Collection, New York

◁ CAMILLE MONET WITH HER DOG, 1866
Oil 29″ × 21″. Emil G. Buehrle Collection, Zurich

13

Sailboats, 1857 (Sketchbook)
Pencil Drawing 8" × 11" Michel Monet Coll. Giverny

sailles. Renoir and Monet were then painting at La Grenouillère. Their pictures at that period bore traces of the main technical characteristics of impressionism, such as separate brush strokes (or " touches " in the painter's jargon), the frequent use of unmixed colours, reflected light, at that time in water, which was the least difficult to interpret. There was also the abandonment of the " light and shade " technique and the rare use of black which was soon to be totally absent from the palette. Although, at this period, Pissarro at Pontoise was developing impressionist techniques and for many years Monet and his friends had held endless discussions on the subject, it is true to say that, at certain periods, all the impressionists played a part in introducing the impressionist style of painting. The mosaicists of very early times had employed the technique of separate brush strokes and minute dashes of colour which go to make up the impressionist's image. The one difference in technique was the use by the ancient mosaicists of very small multi-coloured fragments of stone to provide the dashes of colour in their mosaics. Closer to our own era, the English painter

14

Constable and later Delacroix, under Constable's influence, achieved this colour separation by juxtaposing dashes of colour, each different to its neighbour. Among the impressionists, Delacroix became interested in reflected light in the sense that one colour can very often influence the colour of a neighbouring object just as the colour of an image reflected in a mirror varies from the original.

The impressionists were not the only painters to adopt realism by painting what they saw; Caravaggio. Ribera and Le Nain, for example, strove to achieve this ambition. A contemporary of theirs, Courbet, whom they admired and who was known personally to some of them was also a realist in art.

The first critics to defend the impressionists and explain their art defined it as " painting in light tints ". They believed that the impressionists were the first to reject the technique of light and shade. The fact of the matter was that Courbet, Corot, Jongkind and Boudin had already been producing canvases bathed in light. There had even been artists in the XVI and XVIIth centuries who had used similar techniques. Many pre-renaissance paintings

Sailboats, 1857 (Sketchbook). Pencil Drawing 8″ × 11″. Michel Monet, Coll. Giverny

contain very few shadows and shadows are totally absent in some. In short, impressionism is more a question of regrouping a certain number of processes and methods which had become dispersed than an invention in itself. One can go so far as to say that this regrouping was accomplished by many artists and that it is not possible to single out an individual as responsible for the impressionist style. Bearing in mind the events and sets of circumstances of the time, Monet played a key rôle in the development of the style of painting. It was the degree to which Monet identified himself with his work which, with other manifestations of impressionism gave birth to neo-impressionism and abstract art. It was during the exhibition of Monet's works in the galleries of " La Vie Moderne " in 1880 that the first notions of what to develop four years later into neo-impressionism entered Signac's mind.

Kandinsky, whom many art historians consider as the originator of abstract art never forgot one particular day. While visiting an exhibition in Munich in 1898, he stopped suddenly before a painting and thought – the colours are superb, but there is something disconcerting about the harmony – and he stood for a long time in contemplation before a painting in which the colours alone made a profound impression on him. He felt a deep admiration for the work. On coming to himself he discovered he had no clear idea what the picture represented nor did he know the painter's name. On reading the inscription on the frame, he found it represented a group of haystacks and was signed Claude Monet.

It was, therefore, while Kandinsky was examining one of Monet's canvases that he had, for the first time, the feeling of what a picture representing no really definable object would look like. He had, in fact, experienced his first notions of what abstract art was to offer.

The real importance of Monet's contribution, historically, can be judged when it is viewed in the light of what abstract art was to become. Monet also played a decisive part in the development of impressionism. It was he who decided to organise the impressionist's first exhibition and it was he who was to dominate this group of artists although he had begun to lead them eleven years earlier.

The young painter felt dissatisfied with the useless, conventional form of teaching he received at the studio of Gleyre in 1863. He therefore rounded up three like-minded fellow pupils, Renoir, Bazille and Sisley and announced – " there is no sincerity here: the atmosphere is unhealthy: let's escape ". Instead of taking them to another studio, they set out for the forest of Fontainebleau where they began to paint in the open air. This was nothing out of the ordinary because, at the time, there already were painters who worked out of doors; but for young painters, it was a revolutionary gesture and showed their unwillingness to conform. This step showed up what was to be an essential aspect of the impressionist attitude to art.

When an artist paints a landscape of trees, rocks, ponds, mossy pools of water and an expanse of grass on the spot, he is less likely to invent than if he paints from sketches or in a studio with a teacher. In the open air, what he is to paint lies before him – there is the stirring of leaves and trees in the wind. The shimmering light produces an impression: the young painter was to set great store upon this word. He runs the risk of losing the thread if he

JEAN MONET IN HIS CRADLE, 1867
Oil 45¾″ × 35″   George Friedland Collection, Merion, Pennsylvania

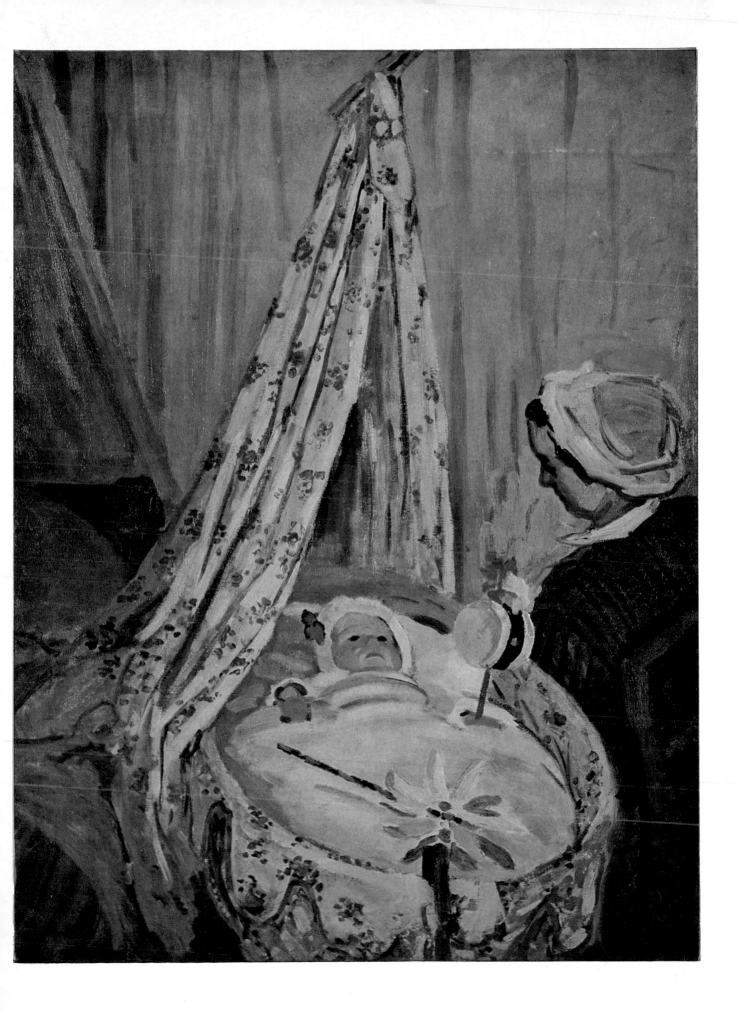

WOMEN
IN THE GARDEN
(Detail), 1867
Oil 97″ × 79″
Louvre, Paris

18

PORTRAIT OF
MADAME
GAUDIBERT
1868
l 85″ × 56½″
Louvre, Paris

19

Michel Monet and Jean-Pierre Hoschedé 1885.
Charcoal on Canvas 28″ × 24″ Michel Monet, Collection Giverny

transfers his ideas to canvas later on. There is more to it than that. The painter cannot rely upon his own deceptive memory which overlooks certain aspects and enlarges upon others. He fails to realise what he has forgotten and he imagines what he thinks he remembers. Errors become embellished by hearsay and discussion and by what he sees around him in the meantime. He consults pictures by artists who see things differently with the result that he thinks he has seen what the artist saw. Has the artist seen shadows in the forest? The painter begins to think that he, too, has seen them and the result is a betrayal of the forest and himself. Our young artists erected their easels among the trees at Fontainebleau in an effort to avoid these two cardinal errors and it was Claude Monet who led them there.

On another occasion, Monet and Renoir were together in Bazille's studio. Their friend had lent it to them in his absence. It was situated in the Place Furstenberg in Paris, opposite the one owned by Delacroix. Renoir and Monet greatly admired Delacroix and were

STILL LIFE, FISH, 1870 Oil 11½″ × 20″
Fogg Museum of Art, Harvard University, Cambridge, Mass.

IMPRESSION: SUNRISE, 1872   Oil 17½″ × 21″   Marmottan Museum, Paris

always on the look-out for news about him. One day they saw a model enter the studio belonging to " the head of the romantic school of painting " as Baudelaire had called him. A few minutes later, the model left. The young painters were very surprised to note how short a time the model had posed for the artist. They talked about it and finally reached two possible conclusions – either Delacroix had studied the model and was to paint her at leisure from memory or he had painted her very rapidly during the short time she had been in his studio. Delacroix died a few weeks later, before they had been able to establish what, in fact, had happened in the studio. It was up to them to decide which of the alternatives was the more worthy of Delacroix. When, in 1874 we see Claude Monet in his boat near Argenteuil, there is no doubt at all as to which method Delacroix had employed.

23

Man Sitting under a Tree, 1857. (Sketchbook)
Pencil Drawing 11″ × 8″ Michel Monet, Collection Giverny

ROCHES NOIRES. HOTEL AT TROUVILLE, 1870
Oil 34½″ × 22″. J. Laroche Collection, Paris ▷

THE RIVER, 1868   Oil 32″ × 39″
Potter Palmer Collection, The Art Institute of Chicago, U.S.A.

La Grenouillère, 1869   Oil 29″ × 39″
H. O. Havemeyer Collection, Metropolitan Museum of Art, New York

THE BEACH AT TROUVILLE, 1870
Oil 15″ × 18″. Tate Gallery, London

28

THE RAPHAEL OF WATER

The man out for a walk along the Seine was still shading his eyes from the sun. He saw the man with the bell-shaped hat draw his oars into the boat and reach for a kind of stool on which he placed a white rectangular object 23½″ wide and 20″ high. The artist then opened the box, took up a slender stick in his right hand and placed the thumb of his left hand in a hole inside an oval-shaped board. The man on the bank at once recognised the painter's tools as he caught sight of each piece of equipment. The stick must be his brush; the board his palette. The box will contain his tubes of paint. Nowadays, these tubes would naturally form part of a painter's equipment, but in 1874, they were a novelty, having appeared on the market for the first time in 1861.

They greatly simplified the physical side of painting. It was now only a matter of unscrewing the cap on the tube and of squeezing the soft metal. Tubes were so much easier to carry about than the powders of days gone by, never easy to deal with outside the studio. It was now possible to use oils out of doors even in a wind such as was blowing across the Seine that day.

REGATTA AT ARGENTEUIL, 1872   Oil 19″ × 29½″   Louvre, Paris

ANEMONES. Oil 15″ × 20″. Private Collection

PORTRAIT OF MRS. HOSCHEDÉ-MONET (The Painter's Daughter). Rouen Museum, Rouen

31

Studies, 1864 (8″ × 9″) Private Collection

Monet extended the legs of his portable easel and set it up on the solid foundation of the boards at the bottom of his boat. His white, rectangular canvas shone in the sun before him. He was, of course, not the first artist to install an easel in a small boat. His friends, Renoir and Sisley had sailed down the Seine nine years previously, in 1865, to watch the Regatta at Le Havre. They had stopped to paint at places on the way down that had attracted them. Earlier, Daubigny, a well-known landscape painter whom the impressionists had met in the forest at Fontainebleau had also painted from his small boat the "Botin". Daubigny had been very helpful to them, especially on one occasion when he had persuaded the Jury of the Salon to accept their canvases and exhibit them.

JEAN MONET ON A MECHANICAL HORSE, 1872
Oil 23½″ × 29″. Nathan Cummings Collection, Chicago

33

MADAME MONET AND HER CHILD, 1875
Oil 21¹/₂″ × 25¹/₂″   Webster Coll., Boston, Mass.

34

THE LUNCH, 1873
Oil 62″ × 78″   Louvre, Paris

MADAME MONET
IN JAPANESE GUISE
1876
Oil 90½″ × 56″
Museum
of Fine Arts
Boston

36

Woman with a Parasol, 1886. Pencil Drawing 21″ × 16″ Private Collection

WOMAN WITH
A PARASOL
1886
Oil 51″ × 34½
Louvre, Paris

WOMAN WITH
A PARASOL
1886
il 51″ × 34½″
Louvre, Paris

But Monet's boat, which the man on the banks of the Seine had called "Monet's workshop", was of more practical use to him than a boat had been to painters in the past. Why should one be surprised that the "Raphael of Water" should paint from a small boat? How often as a child, by the sea, had Monet thought about that fairy land in the water! He was born in 1840 in Paris, but he spent his childhood and early manhood close to the sea. Later he was to say "I want to spend my whole life by the sea and upon its waves: when I die, I want to be buried in a buoy". Eugene Boudin, a painter of sea and sky, discovered that the little caricaturist from Le Havre whose portraits hung in an ironmonger's window, had the makings of a great artist. Monet gave up caricatures which had brought him considerable notoriety and learnt the technique of painting from Boudin. Boudin encouraged Monet to study the technique of recording on canvas the appearance of water, for Boudin was, with Jongkind, another of Monet's friends, one of the most active founders of the school of impressionists. Monet's profound study of water from the landing-stage of La Grenouil-lère was the inspiration for his first impressionist paintings. It must have been Monet who encouraged and inspired Renoir, at this same spot, to erect his easel before this scene whose main attraction was the ever-moving play of sunshine upon the surface of the water.

Monet was forever on the look out for water. When he found himself away from the sea, he went in search of a river or a stream and even canals. He visited Amsterdam in 1880 and Venice in 1909. Both these cities are renowned for their canals. Towards the end of his life, he found satisfaction in a pond which, fortunately, was in his garden. One of the last of his masterpieces "Water Lilies" was inspired by this stagnant pond and its flora.

Monet's feeling for water included water in its many aspects such as the wetness of mist and smoke. The canvas entitled "An Impression: Sunrise" (page 27), denounced in a fit of ill-will by a newspaper man, is not only a seascape but also a study of morning mist. When, between 1876 and 1878, Monet painted his pictures of La Gare St. Lazare (page 43), he emphasised yet another aspect of water–smoke from the locomotives. Again in 1880 when he painted the breaking up of ice, he was describing another aspect of water. He was attracted to and fascinated by what might be called "metaphorical water". He upset what, until then, had been a long-standing habit of artists to paint the sea in "watery" colours. His brush transformed land into water – his meadows have a look of the sea, and his trees take on the appearance of masts. His crowds in the Boulevard des Capucines, dated 1873 might be a seascape. Sometimes the trunks and branches of his trees appear as rivers and streams flowing past a transparent wall.

But to paint ordinary water, its derivatives and watery representations of things did not fully satisfy Monet. He added what might be described as "technical water" to his vision of water in the ordinary sense, to water that had undergone a radical change (the meta-morphosis of water) and to "metaphorical water". This "technical water" is a kind of pictorial affirmation of his techniques for putting on canvas waves and other surface move-ments. He developed this process in the sky at Amsterdam (page 42). The houses in Am-sterdam look like pearls, a technique he adopted by the separation of touches of colour – trees resemble geysers and even his own skin in his self-portrait of 1917 when he was 77

POPPY FIELD, 1873
Oil 19¹/₂″ × 25¹/₂″   Louvre, Paris

41

ST. LAZARE STATION, 1877
Oil 29½″ × 40½″
Louvre, Paris

43

TULIP FIELD
IN HOLLAND
1886
Oil 25½″ × 32″
Louvre, Paris

Dutch Seascape, Holland 1871 (18½″ × 29″) Durand-Ruel Collection, Paris

years old (page 89), he treats, the immobile parts, especially his cheek-bones, as though his skin were composed of minute waves. Rodin, who exhibited with him in 1889 used the same process in his statues and divided up the surface into minute waves. Many other artists adapted the same technique to their own ends. In Monet's work, water was the dominant motif, even as far as the liquification of stone. The most spectacular example of Monet's liquification was when it became applied to architecture. He applied this technique to his pictures of Rouen Cathedral painted between 1892 and 1894 (pages 66 and 67). Water appears to cascade from slits in the blue of the sky. He treated the Doges' Palace in Venice (page 71) in 1904 and Westminster Palace (pag. 74) in 1908 in the same way.

Although this liquification of stone is the most spectacular example of his technique, that of the sky is even more important because of the extent to which the process was later applied. Here he wotked in the opposite direction. Instead of softening what is hard, he hardens, or adds to the density of the most diffuse of all elements, the atmosphere. The sky became a kind of upper ocean which is barely discernible from the lower ocean. This phenomenon comes out in the View of Amsterdam in the Buehrle Collection at Zurich (page 42) and it can be more easily seen in the View of Westminster Palace (page 46). Monet's liquid sky is the intermediate stage between the technique which depicted gaseous light sky and that hard, mineral sky characteristic of Cézanne's work. In many of Monet's works as in those of Cézanne, space became a hard element. Monet's distant views took on the appearance of liquid walls while Cézanne's were solid. Monet shortens distance by using a downward direction on his subject and this cuts out the sky. He painted ships abandoned on the beach during the winter of 1885. He set up his easel on a sand dune so as to be able to see the ships and from this vantage point he could see, in addition to the ships, the beach, a house and the sea spilling in foam over the pebbles. He had to raise his head and change his angle of vision to see the sky and this is why the sky does not appear in the picture (pag. 60). In 1908, he painted the Doges' Palace in Venice, a picture now exhibited at the National Gallery in Washington. The water in the canal is there, but only the lower part of the Palace. The sky, hidden by the walls, is absent. In 1921, five years before his death, Monet could recognise the presence of water in various forms all round him. He had the gift of casting a spell through his magic brush and of converting all things into liquid. But he never had to call upon witchcraft. He had only to look with head lowered at his garden. Water and flowers are down there together. The sky did, however, appear in his "Water Lilies" (1921, Walter Chrysler Collection). But the sky is an image, reflected in the water only and it is seen to have invaded the entire canvas (pages, 78, 79).

If it was Théodore Duret out for a walk by the Seine on a warm summer's day in 1874, watching Monet preparing to paint from his boat, he might have shouted to the white-coated painter – "You are entirely right to paint water, Monet. Three-quarters of the surface of our planet is covered with water – how wrong we are to call it land – how unjust – it should have been called the sea, for all life was born in water".

The Ancients thought of Venus as having been born in the sea. Biological research into the origins of man has shown that the earliest ancestors of mankind were fish rather than apes.

Leon Machon (The Notary), 1856. Charcoal 24″ × 18″
Carter H. Harrison Collection. The Art Institute of Chicago

There is, therefore, an even closer connection between water and the origins of life. The river upon which the cradle containing Moses floated was a womb. The unborn babe is kept alive in water and water is synonymous with unborn life, a kind of Paradise Lost with the traumatism of birth. So, can it be that Monet's watery world in which he shows everything plunged in his own notion of water is a huge womb in which a yet unborn world lies bathed? What the future was to bring weighed heavily upon mens' minds at the end of the XIXth century as it does today and we cannot escape the notion that the future hides an upheaval so all-embracing that our world, compared with the future is comparable to a babe about to be born or even one unborn. Monet painted life unborn and Cézanne life newly emergent. In Cézanne's eyes, images appeared in bas-relief against the flat surface of a wall, newly born and still attached to its mother. Monet saw the future as yet unborn, embraced in pregnancy. In today's art, equal emphasis is given to these two notions, neither of which has reached a higher stage of development than the other.

Monet's watery world may also appear to us as an all-embracing vision of our planet, one-

Sea-Port (Detail) 1874 (24″ × 40″) Private Collection

A View of Amsterdam, Wester Kerk Tower, 1880
Oil $21^{1}/_{2}'' \times 25^{1}/_{2}''$
Wilstach Collection, Philadelphia Museum of Art, U.S.A.

49

STILL LIFE, 1876
Oil 21″ × 29″
Gulbenkian Collection, Lisbon

STILL LIFE, APPLES AND GRAPES, 1880
Oil 25″ × 32″
A. Ryerson Collection. The Art Institute of Chicago, U.S.A.

51

SUNFLOWERS (Detail) Oil 39″ × 32″ Metropolitan Museum of Art, New York

Vase of Nasturtiums 1880 (25″ × 30″) Wildenstein Gallery, New York

quarter earth, three-quarters ocean, upon which a minutely detailed world lies superimposed. Monet's painting can rightly be described as cosmic. His paintings are microcosms containing in their correct proportions dry and liquid elements, making up the world in which we live.

The watery nature of Monet's paintings associate them with a category already described in connection with the works of Cézanne. This category is associated with the mythical Greek god Antæus who reigned over the trees of the forest and the whole vegetable kingdom. It was believed that Antæus was defeated by Hercules who came to realise that his adversary's strength lay in his attachment to the soil. The uprooted planet then died. But as we have seen already, a planet does not owe its existance to soil alone but to water as well and it is due to his love of water that Monet belongs to this category.

In this connection, his art is akin to a variety of styles, themselves containing allusions to the worlds of plants and water. I have in mind gothic art which has given birth to those cathedrals, veritable forests of stone. There is also baroque art with its smooth wave forms. Today's style is drawn from both gothic and baroque which developed between 1895 and 1910 when Monet was between fifty-five and seventy years of age. Anteistical art is utterly different to geometrical and arithmetical art because its strength owes little to reason and much to instinct and spontaneity. Monet said himself – " I paint just as a bird sings ". This idea is one of those from which such instinctive fauvists as Vlaminck drew inspiration.

On a day in 1901, a strong, healthy-looking young man, more the type of a boxer than someone interested in art, walked into a gallery in Paris exhibiting works by Van Gogh. On leaving, he said "I am as attached to Van Gogh as I am to my father". Maurice Vlaminck, the young man who was, to all intents and purposes a boxer, would certainly not have made so shattering a statement if, earlier, he had not learnt to love colours which, as he was to declare, he first saw in Monet's paintings.

Vlaminck painted from instinct, Monet rather less. But certainly both in their own ways were precursors of art in the abstract; Vlaminck, impulsive, was a painter spurred on by instincts within him. Monet painted splashes of colour in the abstract. Their styles were poles apart from what might be called rational or geometric art.

Monet was spontaneous with a leaning towards realism which he acquired from Courbet. This spontaneity, enabling the artist to " paint as a bird in song " is difficult to acquire, but successive generations can contrive to improve upon it by various means. Two years before Monet died, surrealism appeared. This great artist was, nevertheless, able to extract from the new art form one of its aims which might be called the method of " the bird in song " later to become the technique of automatic writing. This impressive effort by Monet was achieved in spite of the wide differences between surrealism and impressionism.

In 1874, a real bird began to sing above the man on the bank of the Seine who raised his head and looked away from Monet's boat. When he looked back, he began to think of a title to give to the white coated painter – it was to be " The Raphael of Water ".

The symbolism of water in Monet's painting brings to mind the sea voyages of the second half of the XIXth century which were more easily undertaken and longer than hitherto and

Tree Trunks, 1857 (Sketchbook)
Pencil Drawing 11" × 8" Michel Monet Collection, Giverny

which, if they did not alter man's notion of what water really was, they at least altered his ideas about it. Long-distance sea voyages were no longer the perquisite of specialists. Duret, the art critic, actually made a world tour. Before him, Baudelaire had been to India and Pissarro to the West Indies. A year before the first impressionist exhibition, Degas went to live for a few months in New Orleans. Later Gaugin sailed, as Cézanne put it " over all the world's seas ". Finally, the stroller along the Seine, watching Monet in his floating studio was an apprentice in a training cargo boat at the age of 17 and had sailed for six months between Le Havre and Brazil.

Monet had not made such long sea voyages but he had done more than contemplate the sea at Le Havre during his early years and adolescence. He had crossed to London in 1870 and, a few months later, was to sail across the North Sea to Holland. In 1875, he visited Cézanne at Aix in company with Renoir and he also visited the coast. The following year, he stayed at Bordighera on the Mediterranean sea where he painted studies of light and shade upon leaves and the shimmering waves mirrored in the windows of houses on the shore (page 58). Ten years later, he visited Belle Isle on the Atlantic coast of Canada and in 1909 he stayed at Venice on the Adriatic. So, the sea was not new to him – he had known about it from his very early years.

In 1860, Monet as a young soldier had crossed to Algeria in a cargo boat. He returned to France two years later. One cannot help wondering whether these two trips across the Mediterranean had as much influence upon him as the sea had on Delacroix whose voyage to Morocco and Algeria in 1832 had been the most important event in his life. There is little likelihood of this for thirty years separated the two return trips to France and much had changed in the meantime. But Delacroix had already felt the change that Monet had recognised to a considerable extent. Even the sea seemed different – it was not so completely opposite to the land as it was before. Pascal had already noted that rivers and streams, seas and oceans had become links between continents rather than obstacles separating them. The water covering the globe had taken over from the land as a means of communication. This is what Monet had in mind when he turned stone into water, for although water is now no longer, as substance, entirely opposite to land, the contrary is true; stones are no longer very far removed from water. Cézanne expressed the same idea, but he saw the sea as contaminated by the land. Cézanne's Mediterranean appears as a kind of tarred road. In both cases, however, the same conclusion is reached. There was now far less difference between the aspect of the land and the sea.

Differences between people of various civilizations and the distances separating them were now much less than they had been before. This is what Delacroix realised in the course of his trip to Morocco and Algeria thirty years before Monet went there. In 1832, Delacroix travelled in a part of the world where Europeans had rarely set foot except as prisoners of the Moors and it was said that only as prisoners could they live there. If they valued liberty more than their faith they had to abandon their beliefs and live as renegades. But in Morocco and Tunisia, Delacroix sacrificed nothing. He lived in total freedom as though the two civilizations had ceased to be incompatible and all antagony between them gone forever.

FIELDS IN SPRING, 1887
Oil 30″ × 36½″ Staatsgalerie, Stuttgart

57

BORDIGHERA, 1884   Oil 25½" × 32"
Potter Palmer Collection, The Art Institute of Chicago, U.S.A.

THE CLIFF WALK. POURVILLE, 1882
Oil 25½″ × 32″
Lewis L. Coburn Collection, The Art Institute of Chicago, U.S.A.

Boats in Winter Quarters, Etretat, 1885
Oil 27″ × 32″
Charles H. and Mary F. S. Worcester, The Art Institute of Chicago, U.S.A.

60

The strong opinions which people often acquire from travelling pass from the subconscious to the conscious by roundabout ways. Delacroix was not fully conscious of the disappearance of antagonism between human beings, but he expresssed in his diary his ideas on the optical relationship between visible objects. He wrote – " when we look at ordinary, everyday objects which we see around us in a landscape or within a house, we cannot escape the fact that the atmosphere acts as a link between such objects and that reflected light is the agent binding all things harmoniously together ".

One of Claude Monet's aims was to bring out this association between objects which to him symbolised the associations between civilizations and the gradual reduction of natural frontiers such as seas and oceans. Delacroix's diary of 1857 included notes on his discovery of the relationship between separate objcects which was to be of such great significance. Dawn was breaking...

The River at Liancourt.
Oil on Canvas 21" × 26" The Portland Art Museum, Portland. Oregon

SUNRISE

The sun rose slowly in the mist enveloping Le Havre. Monet was watching it from behind his window. He felt overjoyed at the sight of what he saw before him. He saw the water and the fog creating unity out of diversity which had meant so much to Delacroix and over everything, the sun, a symbol of the future yet unborn within the present, floating upon the mist like an unborn child in its mother's womb. This vision of a ball of light held captive within a misty, watery, world was to haunt him until the end of his life, when, as an old man he would paint in his garden at Giverny the reflection of clear sky in the greenish blue water in a pond.

But today, Monet is a young man at the age of thirty-six just starting out on his career as an impressionist painter, but already with much accomplished. The slowly rising sun symbolises the story of his gradual mastery of clarity in art. Responsible for this discovery was a side of his character, a fundamental human quality or an attitude of mind without which, the view he was contemplating, would have much lost of its subtlety.

It is understandable that Monet's landscape " An Impression: Sunrise " (page 23) caused an upheaval, for although we may have little difficulty in understanding many of the reasons

IMPRESSION SUNRISE

Boats on the Tamise, 1902   Barbier Collection

Cl. M. 1902

The Port of Touques, 1865 Charcoal Private Collection, New York

why Monet was interested in this particular site for a painting, things were different in 1874 when this canvas was exhibited.

It is a remarkable example of a class of simple painting which has only recently become important. The reason for this is that nowadays we are so swamped with pictures, bright colours, all that the cinema, television, illustrated papers, coloured posters, photographs and simplified travelling can offer that we have become exhausted by the incessant turmoil of modern life. We crave for peace and quiet. This picture epitomises our needs. We see an orange-coloured sphere, three minute barges, one of which is barely visible, a few lines indicating waves and a limited range of tints. We feel attracted to a picture with few embellishments. The outsides and interiors of houses are presented in all their simplicity as they were in days gone by. Through this contrived simplicity of detail and form our imagination is given a chance to develop away from overcharged superabundance.

Our imagination comes to life again just as the day dawned over Le Havre. We feel it stir before the sight of the sun struggling to pierce the mist just as Monet was stirred and fascinated and with him, we gradually discover the real wealth of sea and landscape which, at first sight, seems so barren. The position of the warm-coloured sphere in the picture is of particular interest. Monet painted it on the right of his picture rather than in the centre and thereby added a note of originality. The sphere is minute and reminds one of the Japanese master-engraver Hokusaï whose unrealised ambition was to produce a single dot so perfectly executed and situated on a page that it appeared to be alive. If Hokusaï were to succeed in his ambition, an essential requirement would be a public sufficiently aware to understand his meaning. There have been, for centuries, people in the Far East able to understand Hokusaï's ambition, especially from among an elite class of Buddhists who find that simple paintings help in their metaphysical meditations and mystical research. Could Monet have been a mystic after the zen(ital) monks or Chinese and Japanese contemplative painters? A great deal of thought has been given to this question for a long time. There is no doubt that he was conversant with the work of the masters of Japanese engraving, for a shop selling Chinese and Japanese objects had been opened in 1862 in the rue de Rivoli. Monet painted a picture in 1876 entitled "The Japanese Girl" (page 36). The model in Japanese dress against a fan-shaped woven background of blue poses in an attitude similar to figures found in etchings of the period of the Empire of the Rising Sun. By a curious coincidence, Monet uses the same words to describe Japan and the title of the picture is identical with that given to etchings. The name will be instrumental in the choice of the word "impressionist".

What seems certain is that, as a mystic, he appears to have achieved the prodigious feat of discovering the infinite in the world around him. The well-known art historian Elie Faure describes this idea of the infinite with these words – one hundred thousand – when he wrote "for Claude Monet, there are 100,000 possible images in the space of a second". This infinite variety of expression is present in the countryside round Le Havre. When I went there for the first time I saw mist surrounding a point of orange light. Later on, I became conscious of barges. I first noticed only the largest of the barges and I saw at once that there were two people on board, one very carefully and economically painted was rowing with a stern oar leaving no doubt about the direction taken by the barge. The other passenger... but was he really a passenger? The other object might have been anything, a sack perhaps, I do not remember because at that moment I began to examine the second barge. I, first of all, thought that, in this one, there were three people and then I remembered the sack in the other barge. Perhaps there were two sacks and an oarsman in this barge or two oarsmen and a sack or even three passengers and a small sail. I was uncertain once again. I then began to look at the third barge: again it seemed mposible to tell whether it was full or empty, still or moving, large or small. I pondered over all the possibilities that it was large, small, moving, stopped, full, empty. I then began to think that the three barges were in a straight line, that if the right-hand one were transposed, it would meet another straight line formed by the reflection of the sun in the water. This produced an angle. If the opposite ends were extended upwards, they would form a triangle. If the orange-coloured point was included, a second triangle would be formed. If various other lines which I then began to notice were extended, such as reflections, sails, masts and cranes which could then be distinguished more clearly in the mist than I had at first thought, a whole host of geometric shapes became visible. This was surprising in so hazy a scene.

Algerian Landscape, 1860-62   Pencil Drawing 5″ × 9″ Michel Monet Collection, Giverny

Then, before I had finished counting them, I became interested in the colours. The sea was not of the same bluish shade all over, but green in certain parts of the picture, yellowish or violet elsewhere, that the sky was of different reddish hues, that the waves were not shown by small monotonous horizontal lines, that some of the lines were thick, others thin, some short, some long, some oblique, some were rigid, others seemed fluid like shoals of fish. I thought of counting them, but gave this up. Here again, as elsewhere in the picture, I found myself up against uncountable elements in touch with the infinite. Each time I noticed or discovered something or even thought so, I found that the opinion I had formed of the whole became modified and I began to think that Elie Faure was right when he spoke of the number of images created by Monet per second as a hundred thousand. This amounted to infinity.

But this infinity might pass unnoticed. To really experience it, one must employ that state of mind recommended to mystics, to art lovers and many other classes of people in a variety of circumstances which, in its highest degree, was one of Monet's fundamental qualities, care and attention.

When the man by the Seine near Argenteuil looked at Monet dressed in white overalls, squatting down on the deck of his floating studio like a tiny Chinese or Japanese sage in a minute boat painted at the base of one of their tinted drawings, Monet is there with brushes in his right hand and his palette in his left. The canvas shines white before him.

ROUEN
CATHEDRAL
MAIN ENTRANCE
1894
Oil 42″ × 28½
Louvre, Paris

ROUEN
CATHEDRAL
AT SUNSET
1894
Oil 41½″ × 25″
Museum
of Fine Arts
Boston, Mass.

He is not painting but concentrating upon the work he is about to start.

Many different thoughts come into his mind while he was sitting by his easel near the window of his room in Le Havre watching the misty sunrise over the harbour. When his thoughts recede and his mind quiets within him, he takes up his brushes and palette. Before he starts working, he ensures that he will be able to detect the slightest movement in the morning haze and reflections in his window pane. These will then be traced upon his canvas with his usual care and attention.

He has still yet to start. He begins to think about a visit he paid to Paris a few months previously in company with his friend Boudin. He was little more than a child when he first met Boudin and was drawing caricatures. Even at that time, his attention was well developed. Nothing escaped him; the slightest defect in a face, a trace of a smile, the way an eyelid dropped and rose again, a bump on the nose, the way lips curled, the shape of eyelids, the curve of a beard or a moustache. His work was much appreciated by those who knew him and he might, one day become a portrait painter. Boudin began to exert influence on him and he turned to landscapes. As his master was forever busy painting a sky, the sea, beaches, sites where water and light are the main elements, Monet was drawn to realise that the three principal elements in daylight as against light in a studio or within a room are – intensity, diffusion and mobility.

How can a moving element be painted? He got his answer in 1860 when he met a man whom he and Boudin had visited. Gustave Courbet the leader of the realist school of painters was in prison, accused of demolishing the Vendome column in Paris. Monet wanted to express to him his sympathy, admiration, friendship and gratitude, for he was very fond of Courbet. It was from him that Monet had learnt an aspect of his style which distinguished him from other impressionists. This was his "expansive style" to be traced in Monet's vigorous brush strokes seen on paintings following his meeting with Courbet. They are evident in " Side of Beef " of 1864 (page 9), his dog's pelt in the 1866 painting (page 12), the head-dress of the woman looking at Jean Monet in his cradle in 1867 (page 17), the grass on which the woman is sitting and looking at " La Rivière " in the 1868 painting. In 1869, two artists were painting the same boat on the Seine, the same shimmering water at " La Grenouillère " (page 27). One of the painters' strokes are round and soft, the other's are straighter and more energetic. The former was Renoir's brushwork, the latter that of Monet, inspired by Courbet. We meet these strokes again in " The Beach at Trouville " painted in 1870 (page 28) and " The Regatta at Argenteuil " of 1874 (page 29) and in " Boats in Winter at Etretat " of 1885 (page 60). The sense of space, particularly, is there in the breath-taking colours of the weeping willows which Monet painted at the end of his life. As time goes by, the various effects of his style become evident.

First, come his spacious brush-strokes which seem to change the very elements of which the picture is composed. The change which comes about on parts of the canvas depends in its intensity, upon whether one is studying it close to or from a distance. When studied close, there is a mysterious element which comes from the very hairs of the brush. When looked at from a distance, what stands out is the fat from the side of beef, the folds in a

BELLE-ISLE-EN-MER, THE ROUGH SEA
Oil 24″ × 29″   Ishibashi Collection, Tokio

69

TWILIGHT OVER VENICE, 1908
Oil 29″ × 36½″   Ishibashi Collection, Tokio

THE DODGES' PALACE AT VENICE, 1908
Oil 24½″ × 23″
Chester Dale Collection, National Gallery of Art, Washington, D. C.

POPPY FIELD NEAR GIVERNY, 1885
Oil 26″ × 32½″ Museum of Fine Arts, Boston

head-dress and the appearance of grass. This elemental change in the picture adds a particular charm, an element of surprise which, according to Baudelaire, has been essential to
man from the earliest times. By employing this style of brushwork, particularly towards
the end of his life, even when the change is not produced when the picture is studied at a
di tance, when the colour remains simply colour without any other significance – grass,
cloth or reflected light, Monet shows that he is painting what really exists. In other words,
we do not recognise everything in the world around us. Sometimes, familiar objects are
barely recognised as such – for example, his weeping willows, painted in the 1920's (page 92).
They have the appearance more, of geysers, green flames, or a waterfall than of trees.
Monet certainly does not attempt, systematically, to paint ambiguously as non-figurative
painters nowadays do, particularly abstract painters who find perpetual inspiration in nature. Monet is in no way envious of them nor does he consider them as unworthy of their

The Banks of the Seine 1878 (21″ × 26″) Durand-Ruel Collection, Paris

profession. Courbet's style was a means of discovery for Monet whose wide brush-strokes brought him closer to reality. These aspects of Monet's style are often fleeting – briefly recognisable after a few seconds' meditation. Great speed in execution is essential, for they must be painted during the period of a few seconds before they are recognised. The technique of spacious brushwork solves the problem of movement as Monet sees it – for it can be painted at speed.

Fishermen at Poissy 1882 Pencil Drawing 10″ × 13½″
J. Sachs Collection, Fogg Art Museum, Harvard University, Cambridge, Mass.

THE INVENTION OF COLOUR

Night has fallen. The little boats cruising near Monet's floating studio come to a stop and the reflection of their sails is just perceptible in the rise and fall of the river water. The man on the bank of the Seine erects the wooden instrument that he has just lain on the grass. There is movement in Monet's boat as his right arm which had, until now, lain on his knees suddenly straightens as it comes to life. There follow in quick succession one – two – three – four – forty – one hundred strokes of the brush. Very quickly, his white canvas is covered with light shades of colour. Monet accomplishes in a few minutes what others would have taken several days or even weeks to paint.

The reason why he works fast is no secret – for according to Baudelaire, when a young artist asked Delacroix's advice, he replied – " Sir, if you are incapable of painting a work-man falling from a roof during the time he is in the air, you are not capable of much ".

It is a relief to know that, at this moment, there are no workmen falling from roofs! When there is a breath of wind with the reflections of shimmering sails, one solution would be to rely upon memory and imagination to capture this fleeting moment. Not so Monet who refuses to paint from memory.

" I paint only what I can see. I have never seen an angel so I shall never paint one ". It was Courbet who held these extreme views and for the past twenty years had scandalised the world of art with his realism. The ageing Ingres once said, dryly, of Courbet – " he is nothing more than one big eye ". Years went by and Cézanne said of one of his colleagues – " he is nothing more than an eye – but what an eye! " and it was Monet.

Monet and Courbet, who were described in similar terms by people with differing views on art, were born to get on well together and to paint in friendly rivalry. As a realist painter, Monet was to surpass Courbet. A glance at the canvas that Monet is painting so rapidly (page 29) at once reveals the influence of Courbet. The energetic movements of his hands as he paints, the sails reflected in the water are those of Courbet. Each stroke of the brush is sure and painted with a solid rectangular movement. The authority of Courbet is there, for both men share a remarkable gift – they are sure of their mission and their ability to accomplish it. They are sure of the need for realism in their painting. Courbet was no idealist. When ideals are mentioned, Courbet paints the ugliest object he can think of. Why so violent an expression of anger? Because, to him, an idea is far poorer, far more insignificant, less mysterious a conception than reality. It was in 1894 that Monet painted the sailing boats moored to the banks of the windless Seine. Nine years dreviously, Pasteur, for the first time, healed a man stricken with rabies, and exploded the myth of spontaneous generation. At this time, also, Courbet ridded art of symbolic angels which, to him, were pure imagination. When Pasteur was discovering the existence of microbes, Monet and the impressionists were discovering what was the real colour of shadows, how the colour of objects varies in reflection, how colours reacted upon each other, how far they penetrated within each other or remained separate. Many complex discoveries, at that time, modified what had, hitherto, been thought to be true. Monet and his associates were quickly overtaking their master Courbet in matters of realism.

Courbet followed the development of Monet's technique with impassioned interest. When Monet painted his friend Bazille, Courbet was there to watch his disciple at work. Monet then painted " Picnic Lunch " in the forest of Fontainebleau and Courbet again was there to discuss techniques with Monet. On another occasion, in 1867, Monet was sitting on the edge of a trench dug in his garden to enable him to paint the upper parts of a canvas on which he was painting four women in light dresses among the leaves. Courbet arrived on the scene apparently unimpressed by the trench, but very surprised to see Monet doing nothing. "What are you doing sitting there – why not work rather than twiddle your thumbs? – there is a lot to do to the picture yet ". Bur Monet shook his head " No, I am waiting for the sun ". A cloud at that moment had concealed the sun and altered the intensity of the light and shadows. The whole picture and objects around it were lifeless without the sun. A shadow had all but hidden a skirt in the picture. The woman sitting with a sunshade in

Boats on the Beach 1864 Charcoal 7" × 12" A. E. Goldschmidt Collection, Stamford, Connecticut

her hand was barely visible. Sunshine was essential if Monet was to capture the true effect (page 18). Later, speaking of Monet, Berthe Morisot was to remark "When I am enjoying one of Monet's pictures I always know instinctively which way to point my open sunshade". So many details, many of which concern the direction of shadows show clearly from which direction the light is coming, where the sun stood in the sky and the time of day.

Courbet had no reason to disapprove of Monet's scruples, for he had only recently been visited by an artist who, on seeing a seascape said – "Mr. Courbet, you have painted a splendid seascape". But Courbet turned a deaf ear. He never liked being congratulated on aspects of his painting which he did not consider he merited. " The sea – the sea? " he asked " I did not paint the sea – it was one o'clock, you understand, one o'clock ".

Though Courbet well understood where Monet's ambitions lay, he was, nevertheless, worried by certain aspects of his style, particularly with regard to the results they were likely to give. Although he was in favour of painting landscapes out of doors, he was against painting portraits outside the studio. Facial features need to be painted with great care. Only the studio can offer the required equipment. Steady and regular light is essential.

To Courbet, nature and man remained separate. Monet, on the other hand was conscious of the need to unite them. To him, the same sunlight shines on women in a garden and on their footprints in the sand, on boughs of trees and grass. To Courbet, as to other classical painters, and still more to the primitives, there is a certain hierarchy to follow. To

WATER LILIES   Oil 78″ × 234″

Monet, this was not so. It was, to him, not so much a revolution as a new stage in a paint-er's development. In Byzantine and Roman art, the human face and the representation of the diety in human form are given pride of place. Nature studies and landscapes were of little significance in these paintings. Landscapes return, however, in works by pre-renaissance and renaissance artists. Even so, until the emergence of impressionists, por-traits of the human face were prominent. This situation was not altered by Cézanne and the cubists. The human face disappeared in abstract art, to be replaced by a kind of enig-matic landscape with neither horizon nor depth of perspective. Artistic development did not end there. There followed in this mysterious landscape a curious human image, a new kind of man. Monet's research continues, but in a new direction, in an effort to unite the human image and the landscape, and it is perhaps this influence which makes today's research so exciting.

Monet felt his way, hesitatingly, perhaps. He did not make many experiments for he possessed an intuition which was to be his guide: a need to express light. He needed

to see clearly so as to find a solution to the task of uniting man and his universe. For centuries, this problem does not seem to have troubled painters in the western world. Those in the Far East were concerned with it from early times. The results they reached were akin to impressionism in which the image and open air sunlight became fused. The Japanese found a vehicle for their expression in the cultivation of their gardens which, in their pictures, seem literally to enter their homes. In this connection, it is interesting to note that Monet's first picture of individuals and a landscape, painted out of doors, was done in a garden in 1867 and called "Women in a Garden" (page 18).

Soon after my arrival in Japan, I heard Japanese intellectuals whom I was in touch with talk about a fundamental idea which can be expressed in two words – sabi and wabi. The nearest approximation in English of these words is – rust and the hermit's solitude. I understood the deep meaning of these two words only after several talks. It now seems that what is expressed by these two words is clearly connected with Monet's experience. The hermit's solitude applies to Monet. All his biographers agree that he was taciturn by nature

Seascape (*Detail*) 1882 (24″ × 36″) P. T. Wirksen Collection, Buffalo, U.S.A.

WISTERIA (Detail) 1918-1920. 78" × 59" Granoff Collection, Paris

and silent. This is to be expected, for an all-seeing eye is a rare being with little time for conversation. What is known of Courbet does not invalidate this idea, for most of his statements and actions were misinterpreted – so, as Cézanne had suggested, Monet was some thing of a hermit since he was an all-seeing eye. Nor does the fact that he was a leader invalidate my assertion, for one can be both a leader and be spiritually lonely. This Monet, lonely as he was, saw those around him as different to himself as objects of fiction. He acquired this view of mankind when he was a young man – the caricaturist's view contains a streak of cruelty which springs from the feeling that there is no common ground between the caricaturist and his subject. Monet had little sympathy for the Le Havre people whom he ridiculed in his drawings. What the Japanese called rust was what made Monet more humane later on.

Amsterdam, Boats on the Canal   1871   E. Rouart Collection

Mill at Zaandam   1871 (8″ × 16″) R. von Hirsch Collection, Basel

It was the light in Monet's work, particularly when he came to maturity as a painter which acted as rust – it smoothed and rounded the edges, dissolved them and reduced them to dust, a dust composed of tiny splashes of colour – they were reduced to becoming the component parts of tiny waves. But, in reality, it was an extension, for the dividing line between people and things in his works disappeared and people merged imperceptibly into the framework of his designs. The figures were no longer men and women, they became part of the atmosphere surrounding them, the ground upon which they stood. There was a basic divergence between Courbet and Monet in the matter of feet upon the ground. When I first saw Courbet's pictures, I was troubled by what I took to be an error of judgement. I could not place it exactly, but gradually and by dint of careful examination I reached my conclusion which was confirmed many years later. Courbet's characters do not appear to be standing on the ground. They may be as little as one millimetre above but this is sufficient to show clearly that, for example, " The Girls on the Banks of the Seine " are not really lying on the grass. In " Good Day, Mr. Courbet ", the soles of Mr. Bruyas's shoes are not in contact with the sand. Even though those who disapprove of angels in paintings find it an unpalatable truth, the art collector from Montpellier is suspended a fraction above the earth as though he were an angel. Supernatural phenomena of this sort never appear in Monet's work. His people are firmly implanted on the ground. Their

The Blue Train: Water Lilies, 1918-1920. Oil 78" × 59". Granoff Collection, Paris

Haystack, 1893 (26" × 40") Museum of Fine Arts, The James Philips Gray Collection, Boston, Mass.

legs are properly joined to their feet and so on up to their heads which are not detached from the sky which is, itself, one with the sea and the land. In the words of the surrealists, Monet's work is a vast kaleidoscope of communicating vessels by which Monet brings other humans into his world.

To reach them, the universe must first be crossed and for Monet, communicating channels of all sorts must be perfect. While in Courbet's work as in paintings by the majority of western artists until the impressionists, all that is needed for an understanding between the characters in a picture and the viewer to be assured is an accurate flesh tint or correct anatomy. In the west, human relations are based upon a kind of sensual equilibrium or charity in a religious sense, but in the Far East, this conception is almost entirely unknown. Many aspects of his work seem to suggest that Monet was not born in Paris, had not spent his early years at Le Havre but that he had been born and brought up in China or Japan.

He is working in his boat at Argenteuil as speedily as those Japanese writers I have seen covering vast surfaces of paper with signs in under 15 seconds. How many mountains, rivers and rocks have been drawn in Japan or China at the rate at which Monet works! Far Eastern artists achieve lightening speed as do certain contemporary painters of moving objects. Both must avoid including reflections in their pictures which might reduce the rapidity of their work and slacken their creative impulse. This is precisely why Monet drew attention to the connection between his painting and a bird in song. He had to ensure that the reflections he painted did not falsify what he saw. But Monet and the Ear Fastern (particularly Japanese) traditions of painting part company on the question of colour, for Japanese etchings in their bright colours are a high spot in the country's artistic history.

I was, to start with, very surprised to read " the inventor of colour ", a phrase that André Lhote applied to Monet -- " the father of the impressionists " and " the inventor of colour ". I had always preferred the expression " the inventor of light " – but on looking more closely at the question, I realise that Lhote was right. When I saw a well-known group of Monet's water lilies exhibited in Paris (in the Circular Gallery of the Orangerie in the Tuilerie Gardens), I became aware that it was colour rather than light that was the mainspring of my impression. The same applies to cathedrals where colours dominate rather than light. In the "Westminster Palace " series (page 74), it is again colour with its violets, oranges and greens. In the " Twilight Over Venice " (page 70) it is the yellow breaking out in the midst of the blue and the violet within the yellow. Monet's unsurpassed paintings in luminous colours, such as the two equally fine versions of "Women with Sunshade " in the Musée du Jeu de Paume (pages 38 and 39) are good examples of his quite exceptional skill. He did not approve of the neo-impressionists Seurat and Signac and the earliest of the impressionists, Pissarro, who was utterly haunted by light so bright that it outshone his colour. It was the disparity between light and colour that Monet never forgave.

A craving for open-air light was the mainspring of Monet's artistic development and that of other impressionists. Monet began by portraying the intensity of light by showing the contrast between bright light and dark shadow. This is clearly seen in the portrait of his future wife Camille (page 12) and " The Side of Beef " (page 9) in which the light coloured

Scene of Rouen   1872 Pencil Drawing 12″ × 18½″ Clark Art Institute, Williamstown, Mass.

fat stands out against a dark brown background. Contrasts are again evident in " Picnic Lunch " (page 5). Such contrasts of colour, however, prevented him from expressing the diffuse, all-embracing elements of light in the open air. Faced with this problem, he showed a glimpse of his genius. Rather than concentrate upon contrasts of light and shade, he set out to find opportunities out of doors and in his studio to repeat his vision of light. In later years, many artists were to remember this side of his art in their efforts to bring out a true understanding of the subtlety of light. It was now that Monet's son was born. Little Jean lay in his cradle, meditating with a serious air, while a woman in a white hat watched over him. His father noticed that everything about the cradle, sheets, white head-dress, the colour of the nursery walls, the child's toys, were all white. He erected his easel at once and set to work (page 17). The same patters was repeated in " The Lunch " (page 20). Bright sun penetrated light-coloured curtains across the window. There is light throughout the room, accentuated by the white table-cloth, the child's napkin, his blond head, the straw on the chairs and the maid's white head-dress. Parts of the room are dark, but the painter is limited to what he can make use of. Madame Gaudibert is painted in light tints against a light background (page 19). A *clair-obscurist*, whose main preoccupation is not to paint the maximum amount of light, would have substituted a black cloth for the light blue tapestry so as to bring out the luminous silhouette. But Monet was of the opinion that a greater intensity and truer light is obtained by repeating light than by a direct comparison with shadows.

He went further than this and attempted to do away with relief. Shadows must have their counterpart in shafts of light to obtain the effect of volume. The amount of space allotted to light on the canvas is less than that allotted to shadows. Monet made a conscious effort to get rid of them as can be seen on the dresses of the women in " The Beach at Trouville " (page 28) where relief is almost totally absent as is also the case with the womens' dresses in " Picnic Lunch " (page 5). But " Picnic Lunch " is a title which is not really Monet's: it was used by another famous painter at about the same period.

While Monet was at work painting the river Seine at Argenteuil from his boat, the man on the bank had erected his easel and canvas and is painting Monet's boat and the artist aboard it. When he has finished, he will sign the canvas "Manet", a surname not far removed from his model's.

Manet owed much to Monet. It was thanks to Monet that Manet was bold enough, at certain times, to paint without concern for the portrayal of volume. Monet was one of the first painters in the West to have almost entirely ignored it, particularly in his famous " Picnic Lunch " and in his less well-known " Olympia". At this period, Manet was still painting light and shade, dark figures upon a clear background or vice versa. But when the pupil became a master, it was Monet who was to inspire Manet. On this famous day, upon the river bank at Argenteuil, Manet painted Monet in the manner of Monet, the impressionist.

It is established that the impressionistes, including Monet, substituted shadows by colours. But earlier, Rubens had reached the same result in company with certain mosaicists. One of the great innovations which coincided with the birth of the impressionist school was painting of light reflected from one object to another which altered the colour of objects to such an extent that the painter's original intention is often in doubt. Everything depended upon what objects were depicted on the canvas near the light reflections. It is true that owing to reflected light and the special use artists made of it, a general fusing of light resulted which was, probably, more complete than it had ever been before. At the same time, composition was no longer of any importance.

The effect of this becomes apparent when two of Monet's portraits are compared. One was executed during his pre-impressionist period (the portrait of Madame Gaudibert dating back to 1868, (page 19) and the other is the impressionist portrait of Madame Hoschedé-Monet (page 31). In the portrait of Madame Gaudibert, (page 19) Monet takes practically no notice of reflected light. In the luminous atmosphere, shapes stand out clearly while at the same time, there is a risk of a clash. The artist must manage to reconcile a table with a human form, the conical shape of a dress with the plane surface of a wall. Monet does this supremely well. But he had to ask Madame Gaudibert to lay her gloved hand in such a way as to allow the whiteness of the glove to be repeated in the whiteness of the collar, to stand in a three-quarters position so that the start of her shoulder curve should be in a

SELF-PORTRAIT, 1917. Oil $27^1/_2'' \times 21^1/_2''$. Louvre, Paris

straight line with the fold of the blue curtain. In short, all manner of preparations were necessary, a veritable display of the art of composition.

When, much later, Monet painted his daughter, Madame Hoschedé-Monet, (page 31), all this elaborate arrangement was no longer necessary. Harmony is achieved in the picture through the deployment of reflected light. The light is still as intense, but shapes and tints melt into each other. Shadows do not throw up contrasts, nor did their area have to be carefully calculated. The nose shadow is red in a rose-coloured face. The most attentive eye will find the composition sublime throughout. Harmony pervades all through the picture, the universe is nothing more than an area of complete harmony.

But limitless harmony must become imperceptible at last. When all goes well, the general impression is that all has gone too well. I might even go so far as to suggest that there is

Sunset at Port-Villes   1883   (29″ × 36″)   Durand-Ruel Collection, Paris

Haystacks, Pencil Drawing 6″ × 9½″ Private Collection

no way of knowing whether all is well or not. At this point, the real invention of colour enters Monet's work.

The first great colourist of the XIXth century, Delacroix, who admired Monet and of whom Baudelaire so often remarked that he was the inventor of colour, the colourist *par excellence* still concealed his colours in the shadows of light and shade. These colours, in fact, were the colours of the spectrum. But colour is something else besides. Each tint possesses a power and luminosity dissimilar to simple light. Van Gogh felt this when he strove to express passions in terms of red and blue. Kandinsky developed this study which is still far from complete. But when one looks at Madame Hoschedé's red hat and the various tints that go to make up her portrait and one carefully examines all the paintings which bring in the style of Bonnard whom Monet knew towards the end of his life, it becomes clear that of all that goes to make up Monet's undying fame, that of being the inventor of colour is, perhaps, the greatest feat. By achieving this, he brought back into art a challenging note which ensured that his contribution was not to be a vague, optimistic image of a shadowy world, but through the secrets of colour, a mysterious representation of the enigmatic, creative force of life. All this was achieved in the teeth of his most ardent critics whose objections were not that his paintings lacked harmony, but that they contained too much.

Tangled Foliage, 1918-1920. Oil 47″ × 39″. Granoff Collection, Paris

BIOGRAPHY

1840. 14th November: born in Paris – childhood and adolescence spent at Le Havre.

1859. Settled in Paris; attended the Swiss Academy where he became acquainted with Pissarro whom he accompanied on painting expeditions.

1860-61. Did his military service in Algeria in the regiment "Chasseurs d'Afrique".

1862. Returned to Le Havre and spent the summer there with Boudin and Jongkind. He entered the Gleyre Academy in Paris in November where he met Bazille, Renoir and Sisley.

1864. Painted in the Forest of Fontainebleau and at Barbizon.

1865. A seascape of his was accepted by the Salon. He painted "Picnic Lunch" in the Forest of Fontainebleau.

1866. "Portrait of Camille" accepted by the Salon. He met Manet who, with Courbet, exercised an influence upon him.

1868. At Etretat and Fecamp where he attempted suicide.

1869. At Bougival – bathing parties at "La Grenouillère".

1870. His works were refused by the Salon. He married Camille in June and left for England in September.

1871. He met Pissarro again in London and accompanied Daubigny to Holland.

1872. A second trip to Holland; on his return settled at Argenteuil.

1874. He presented 12 canvases, the most important of which was "Impression: Sunrise" at the group's first exhibition.

Boats on the Beach, 1865 Pencil Drawing 9″ × 12″ Private Collection

1878. He settled in the village of Vetheuil with a *pied-à-terre* in Paris.

1883. He went to live at Giverny near Vernon in the valley of the Eure in April.

1884. Stayed at Bordighera from 18th January to 3rd April and at Menton from 8th April to 13th April.

1891. Visited London in the autumn.

1892. He painted " Cathedrals at Rouen ".

1894. An exhibition was held of his series of views of London " Parliament " – " Waterloo Bridge " – " Charing Cross ".

1908. He went to Venice where, as in London, he studied aspects of luminous mists.

1909. The series of "Water Lilies" which was started in 1898 and under revision during the previous four years.

1922. He underwent an operation for cataract which restored his sight.

1926. He died at Giverny on 6th December.

1953. The blurred nature of his paintings led certain theorists to recognise Monet as one of the first to employ the technique of Tachism.

BIBLIOGRAPHY
MAGAZINE ARTICLES

E. TABOUREAUX, *Claude Monet*, La Vie Moderne, June, 12th 1880.

A. DE LOSTALOT, *Exposition des œuvres* de M. Claude Monet, Gazette des Beaux-Arts I, 1883.

O. MIRBEAU, *Claude Monet*, L'Art dans les Deux Mondes, March, 7th.

T. ROBINSON, *Claude Monet*, Century Magazine September, 1892.

M. GUILLEMET, *Claude Monet*, Revue Illustrée, March, 1898.

A. FONTAINAS. *Claude Monet*, Mercure de France, May, 1899.

THIEBAULT-SISSON. *Claude Monet, un entretien*. Le Temps, November, 27th, 1900.

L. VAUXCELLES, *Un après-midi chez Claude Monet*, L'Art et les Artistes, December, 1905.

W. PACH, *Interview with Monet, His Career and Work*, The Studio, March, 1908.

M. E. ELDER, *Chez Claude Monet à Giverny*, Paris, 1924.

DUC DE TREVISE, *Le pélerinage de Giverny*, Revue de l'Art ancien et moderne, January, 1927.

R. KOECHLIN, *Claude Monet*, Art et Décoration, February, 1927.

R. REGAMEY, *La Formation de Claude Monet*, Gazette des Beaux-Arts, February, 1927.

L. C. PERRY, *Reminescences of Claude Monet from 1889 to 1909*, The American Magazine of Art, March, 1927.

R. GIMPEL, *At Giverny with Claude Monet*, Art in America, June, 1927.

P. JAMOT, *A propos de l'exposition Monet*. Bulletin des Musées, 1931.

G. POULAIN, *L'origine des Femmes au jardin de Claude Monet*. L'Amour de l'Art, March, 1937.

F. ARCANGELI, *Monet*, Paragone N. 31, 1952.

G. BACHELARD, *Les Nymphéas ou Les surprises d'une nuit d'été*, Verve VII, 27-28, 1952.

K. H. USENER, *Claude Monets Seerosen-Wandbilder in der Orangerie*, Wallraf-Richartz Jahrb. Cologne 1952.

W. C. SEITZ, *Monet and Abstract Painting*, College Art Journal, I, 1956.

C. GREENBERG, *Later Monet*, Art News Annual, 1957.

MONOGRAPHS

O. MIRBEAU, *Claude Monet, « Venise »*, Paris, 1912.

A. ALEXANDRE, *Claude Monet*, Paris, 1921.

G. GEFFROY, *Claude Monet, His Life, His Time, His Work*, Paris, 1922.

C. MAUCLAIR, *Claude Monet*, Paris, 1924.

F. FELS, *Claude Monet*, Paris, 1925 and 1927.

F. FOSCA, *Claude Monet*, Paris, 1927.

L. GILLET, *Three Variation on Claude Monet*, Paris, 1927.

G. CLEMENCEAU, *Claude Monet, The Water Lilies*, Paris, 1928.

L. WERTH, *Claude Monet*, Paris, 1928.

M. DE FELS, *The Life of Claude Monet*, Paris, 1929.

Lady LATHOM, *Claude Monet*, London, 1931 and New York, 1932.

S. GWYN, *Claude Monet and His Garden*, London, 1934.

G. GRAPPE, *Monet*, Paris, 1941.

H. ROSTRUP, *Claude Monet and His Paintings in Danish Collections*, Copenhagen, 1941.

A. M. CETTO, *Claude Monet*, Basel, 1943 and 1947.

O. REUTERSWAERD, *Monet*, Stockholm, 1948.

C. SCHWEICHER, *Monet*, Berne, 1949.

C. ROGER-MARX, *Monet*, Lausanne, 1949.

C. LEGER, *Claude Monet*, Paris, 1950.

G. BESSON, *Claude Monet*, Paris, 1951.

P. WESTHEIM, *Claude Monet*, Zurich, 1953.

ILLUSTRATIONS